Growing Readers

from

Purchased with Smart Start Funds

Dragonflies

by Cheryl Coughlan

Consulting Editor: Gail Saunders-Smith, Ph.D.

Consultant: Gary A. Dunn, Director of Education,
Young Entomologists' Society

Pebble Books

an imprint of Capstone Press
Mankato, Minnesota

Pebble Books are published by Capstone Press
818 North Willow Street, Mankato, Minnesota 56001
http://www.capstone-press.com

Library of Congress Cataloging-in-Publication Data
Coughlan, Cheryl.
    Dragonflies/by Cheryl Coughlan.
    p. cm.—(Insects)
    Includes bibliographical references (p. 23) and index.
    Summary: Simple text and photographs introduce the physical features
of dragonflies.
    ISBN 0-7368-0238-X
    1. Dragonflies—Juvenile literature. [1. Dragonflies.] I. Title. II. Series: Insects
(Mankato, Minn.)
QL520.C685   1999
595.7'33—dc21
                                                                98-32304
                                                                     CIP
                                                                      AC

Note to Parents and Teachers

The Insects series supports national science standards for units on
the diversity and unity of life. The series shows that animals have
features that help them live in different environments. This book
describes and illustrates the parts of dragonflies. The photographs
support early readers in understanding the text. The repetition of
words and phrases helps early readers learn new words. This book
also introduces early readers to subject-specific vocabulary words,
which are defined in the Words to Know section. Early readers may
need assistance to read some words and to use the Table of
Contents, Words to Know, Read More, Internet Sites, and
Index/Word List sections of the book.

Table of Contents

4

Dragonflies live near water.

Dragonflies can be colorful.

8

Dragonflies have
a long body.

Dragonflies have six legs.

12

Dragonflies have
four wings.

antennas

Dragonflies have
two short antennas.

Dragonflies have
two huge eyes.

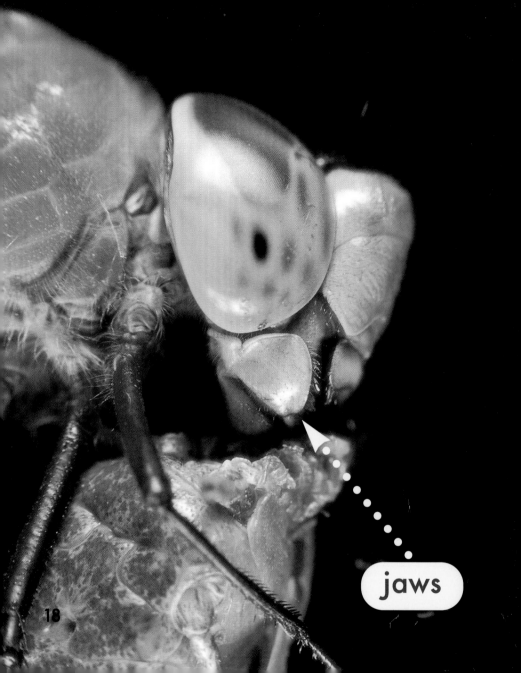

jaws

Dragonflies have strong jaws.

Dragonflies eat
other insects.

Words to Know

antenna—a feeler on an insect's head

eye—a body part used for seeing; dragonflies have large eyes made of many small lenses; dragonflies can see in nearly all directions at the same time.

insect—a small animal with a hard outer shell, three body parts, six legs, and two antennas; insects may have two or four wings.

jaw—a mouthpart used to grab things, bite, and chew; dragonflies use their jaws to catch and eat insects such as flies, gnats, and mosquitoes.

wing—a movable part of an insect that helps it fly; dragonflies have clear, tinted, or spotted wings.

Read More

Gerholdt, James E. *Dragonflies.* Incredible Insects. Edina, Minn.: Abdo & Daughters, 1996.

Haufmann, Janet. *Dragonflies.* Bugs. Mankato, Minn.: Smart Apple Media, 1998.

Merrick, Patrick. *Dragonflies.* Chanhassen, Minn.: Child's World, 1998.

Rice, R. Hugh. *Dragonflies.* Katomah, N.Y.: Richard C. Owen, Publishers, 1996.

Internet Sites

Dragonflies
http://www.eou.edu/~yenneys

Dragonfly: First You See Me, Then You Don't
http://www.letsfindout.com/subjects/bug/rfidragn.html

What about Dragonflies?
http://www.winsomedesign.com/Shrub_Steppe/Dragonflies.html

Index/Word List

antennas, 15
body, 9
colorful, 7
dragonflies, 5, 7, 9,
   11, 13, 15, 17,
   19, 21
eat, 21
eyes, 17
huge, 17
insects, 21

jaws, 19
legs, 11
live, 5
long, 9
near, 5
short, 15
strong, 19
water, 5
wings, 13

Word Count: 39
Early-Intervention Level: 7

Editorial Credits
Mari C. Schuh, editor; Timothy Halldin, cover designer; Kimberly Danger and
   Sheri Gosewisch, photo researchers

Photo Credits
Dembinsky Photo Assoc. Inc./Gary Meszaros, 4
Fred Siskind, 6
GeoIMAGERY/Jim Roetzel, 10
James P. Rowan, cover
Joe MacDonald, 1, 12, 14
Susan Fry, 8
Unicorn Stock Photos/Ed Harp, 16
Visuals Unlimited/Bill Beatty, 18; Mary Meszaros, 20